Machines at Work

Tow Trucks

by Cari Meister

A.C.
CARTER & SON
RECOVERY
Horley, Surrey

Bullfrog
Books

Ideas for Parents and Teachers

Bullfrog Books let children practice nonfiction reading at the earliest reading levels. Repetition, familiar words, and photo labels support early readers.

Before Reading

- Discuss the cover photo. What does it tell them?
- Look at the picture glossary together. Read and discuss the words.

Read the Book

- "Walk" through the book and look at the photos. Let the child ask questions. Point out the photo labels.
- Read the book to the child, or have him or her read independently.

After Reading

- Prompt the child to think more. Ask: Have you ever seen a tow truck? Was it towing anything?

Bullfrog Books are published by Jump!
5357 Penn Avenue South
Minneapolis, MN 55419
www.jumplibrary.com

Library of Congress Cataloging-in-Publication Data
Meister, Cari.
  Tow trucks / by Cari Meister.
      pages cm. -- (Bullfrog books. Machines at work)
  Includes bibliographical references and index.
  Summary: "This photo-illustrated book for early readers tells about the parts of a tow truck and how it works"-- Provided by publisher.
  Audience: Grades K to grade 3.
  ISBN 978-1-62031-048-9 (hardcover : alk. paper) --
ISBN 978-1-62496-060-4 (ebook)
  1. Wreckers (Vehicles)--Juvenile literature. I. Title.
  TL230.5.W74M45 2014
  629.225--dc23   2012042021

Series Editor: Rebecca Glaser
Book Editor: Patrick Perish
Series Designer: Ellen Huber
Book Designer: Sara Pokorny

Photo Credits: Alamy, 5, 10, 14, 16, 22 (main), 24; Corbis, 4; Dreamstime, 13, 23br; iStock, 12, 21; Shutterstock, cover, 1, 3, 8, 15, 18–19, 22b, 23tl, 23tr, 23bl; Superstock, 6–7; Veer, 9

Printed in the United States of America at Corporate Graphics in North Mankato, Minnesota.
5-2013 / PO 1003
10 9 8 7 6 5 4 3 2 1

Table of Contents

Tow Trucks at Work

Oh no!

A car broke down.

Who can help?
A tow truck!

Beep! Beep!

A tow truck backs up.

A driver gets out of the cab.

He pushes a button.

hook ···▶

It unwinds the cable.
The hook comes down.

wheel lift

The driver hooks up the car.
The front wheels rest on the wheel lift.
The back wheels stay on the ground.

Vroom!

Off he goes to the repair shop!

www.theaa.com

AA

AA

RX07 TAU

14

A van is parked in a loading zone.
A tow truck comes to move it.

15

Oh no!

A bus was in an accident.

A big tow truck moves it off the road.

Oh no! A blizzard!
A car went off the road.
A tow truck pulls it out.

LODGING – EXIT 201

Tow trucks are helpful!

Parts of a Tow Truck

cable
A very strong rope made of metal wire.

cab
The place where the driver sits.

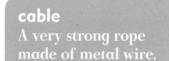

hook
A strong curved piece that attaches the cable to a car for towing.

wheel lift
A metal bar that lifts up the front wheels of cars for towing.

(truck text:) Barnett's Wrecker Service I-40, Hwy. 13, Hurricane Mills, TN DOT# 1815326 931-296-9765 24 Hour Wrecker Service

Picture Glossary

accident
An event that happens without planning it.

loading zone
The place in front of a building where people can load and unload items quickly, but cannot park.

blizzard
A very big snowstorm where it is hard to see.

repair shop
The place cars and trucks go to be fixed.

Index

To Learn More

Learning more is as easy as 1, 2, 3.

1) Go to www.factsurfer.com

2) Enter "tow truck" into the search box.

3) Click the "Surf" button to see a list of websites.

With factsurfer.com, finding more information is just a click away.